<u>Popular Cat Library</u>

# Abyssinian Cat

Judah Track

Published in association with T.F.H. Publications, Inc.,
the world's largest and most respected publisher of pet literature

<u>Chelsea House Publishers</u>
Philadelphia

# CONTENTS

# Popular Cat Library

Abyssinian Cat
American Shorthair Cat
Bengal Cat
Birman Cat
Burmese Cat
Exotic Shorthair Cat
Himalayan Cat
Maine Coon Cat
Persian Cat
Ragdoll Cat
Scottish Fold Cat
Siamese Cat

**Publisher's Note:** All of the photographs in this book have been coated with FOTO-GLAZE® finish, a special lamination that imparts a new dimension of colorful gloss to the photographs.

Reinforced Library Binding & Super-Highest Quality Boards

Library of Congress Cataloging-in-Publication Data

Track, Judah.
Guide to owning a Abyssinian cat / by Judah Track.
p.    cm. — (Popular cat library)
Summary: A guide to the history, feeding, grooming, exhibition, temperament, health, and breeding of Abyssinian cats.
ISBN 0-7910-5457-8 (hc.)
1. Maine coon cat Juvenile literature.    [1. Abyssinian cat. 2. Cats. 3. Pets.]
I. Title. II. Series.
SF449.A28T725          1999
636.8'26—dc21
                                                          99-26002
                                                          CIP

# HISTORY OF THE ABYSSINIAN

Majestically, yet with a ghost-like stealth, Abyssinian cats paced the great temples of ancient Egypt. They were the children of the gods — their earthly reincarnation. They represented all that was good, all that was divine, and were accorded the respect and worship their omnipotent position demanded. Sadly, as romantic a notion as this is and to which some would like to cling to, the reality of the opening sentences is fact only if the word Abyssinian is removed.

It is within human nature to believe that if we can establish an unbroken lineage to something that existed hundreds or even thousands of years ago, it will in some way bestow greater status to the subject of such lineage. There is nothing wrong with this, for it provides interest and pleasure.

However, when fact and fiction are not clearly identified, there is the danger that they may begin to merge and create a distorted view of the truth — to read more into what we see rather than into the historical reality of its creation. The Abyssinian, as the breed we know today, has an ancestry that goes back no further than the 19th century.

Not only is this true, but the breed, far from being Abyssinian, even less Egyptian, was created in the green and pleasant lands of England. It lived not in the homes of the pharaohs but in those of middle and upper class English gentry, which was a comfortable place to be during its formative years.

How do we know that the breed is not the same one that graced the hallowed portals of ancient Egyptian temples? The answer lies in the fact that prior to the 19th century, there weren't actual cat breeds; there were at best breed types. Only with the formation of cat societies were *types* molded into breeds.

While some people consider the Abyssinian to be a descendant of the sacred cats of Egypt, the reality is that the breed was perfected in Great Britain in the late 1800s. It was brought from Abyssinia (now Ethiopia) by a British officer returning from a military expedition. Owners, David and Karen Boyce.

This was done by comparing individuals against the written standards that laid down the criteria distinguishing the breed from its archetypes. Breeding was selectively biased towards producing offspring that met the physical requirements stated in the breed's standard. The same is true for the Egyptian Mau and many other breeds whose owners fondly believe their feline friends are direct descendants, in purebred form, of cats that were venerated thousands of years ago in given countries.

At best, it can be said that there may be a sprinkling of Egyptian genes in the cats we own that were derived from the felines of the pharaohs. But even this is stretching probability to its very limits and could as easily be said of any present breed.

## WHAT IS AN ABYSSINIAN?

To appreciate what makes an Abyssinian a specific cat breed necessitates understanding its coat pattern. From it, we can make logical premises on how the coat pattern was developed to create the magnificent feline we see today. All wild cats display, to a greater or lesser degree, a coat pattern called agouti, which is the banding of the individual hairs in a light and dark manner to create a ticked appearance as the hairs lay partially one over the other.

A second pattern is superimposed on this in most wild-cat species. In these, certain areas of the agouti pattern are modified. The lighter-colored bands of the hairs are darker. This results in the striped pattern called tabby, which you are no doubt familiar with. It is

Abyssinian breeders have tried to remove the tiger-striped pattern as much as possible, leaving only the agouti pattern. However, the striping on the face, legs, and tail is occasionally still seen, as on this blue Aby kitten. Owner, Chantal Lenasseur.

Ruddy and blue Abys owned by Sheila Dentico. In conformation, the Abyssinian resembles the African wild cat.

commonly referred to as "tiger pattern" by some pet owners in America.

There are three recognized tabby patterns: the mackerel, the blotched, and the Abyssinian. In the mackerel pattern, the striping is vertical, slightly curved, and emanating from a dark band running down either side of the back. The stripes may be continuous or broken into bars or spots. There are stripes on the head and circular bands around the legs and tail. In the blotched tabby, the body striping forms whorls. Where they coalesce, blotches of various sizes are formed. This pattern is more commonly referred to in the cat fancy as "classic" tabby. Our interest lies in the third form, called Abyssinian tabby. In this, the stripes are missing from the body, which has the basic agouti ticked pattern, but some striping remains on the face, legs, and tail. Through selective breeding, the striping on these areas in the Abyssinian breed has been considerably diminished, with the objective being to produce a ticked pattern as devoid as possible of stripes.

Whether the removal of leg and tail bands detracts from the image of an Egyptian look-alike breed of the past is debatable, even more so in light of the fact that the uniqueness of the Aby ended with the arrival of a second ticked breed in recent years — the Singapura.

## FROM EGYPT TO ENGLAND

It is generally agreed by archaeologists and zoologists that the process of feline domestication commenced about 4,000 years ago in the Middle East. It was probably a concurrent process in numerous lands of that region. Egypt has become its focal point because the people of that country venerated cats, which became major deities. There are many artifacts that help to establish a chronological table of the various feline divinities.

Accepting Egypt as the center of domestication, it seems logical to assume that the native wild cats of that area are the ones from which domestic cats probably developed. On this basis, the jungle or marsh cat (*Felis chaus*), the European wild cat (*Felis sylvestris*), and its African wild cat subspecies (*Felis s.libyca*) are the obvious choices.

If *sylvestris* is studied, it will be found that from the very obvious mackerel-tabby markings seen in the northerly ranges of the species that there is a steady reduction of these as the distribution extends south and east. In the African wild cat, the body stripes are faint and sometimes missing. This is also true of *Felis chaus*, which has a pelage not unlike that of the Abyssinian. Color also changes from gray to a sandy brown, as the distribution area becomes more arid and desert-like.

Each of these wild species will hybridize, so we will never know for sure if domestic cats are the result of one, two, or more species, although it is of no great concern to the average cat fancier. The interesting point is that we can see that cats of the Abyssinian-tabby type, as well as those of the mackerel and spotted types depicted in wall and tomb paintings, would have existed in Egypt during the period of the pharaohs.

It would, however, be extremely misleading to say they were Abyssinians because it is a term that is correctly appropriate only to the breed we know under that name today. Similarly ticked, sandy cats have existed in all countries where a wild species displaying this genetic pattern has a natural distribution.

The cats of Egypt were transported to many Middle Eastern and Asian countries, as well as to Europe, where the Greek culture was emerging. These cats would hybridize with local, wild, and semi-domestic cats, and the Abyssinian-tabby genes slowly spread across Europe, helped considerably by the Romans, who not only ruled Egypt for many years but much of Europe as well, including Britain.

## THE BIRTH OF THE CAT FANCY

Following the conquest of Britain by the Romans in 43 BC, there was to be 1,930 years before the emergence of a cat society devoted to the development of feline breeds and the hobby surrounding them. During this period, cats from Europe were shipped to all countries of the world by travelers and military expeditions. Likewise, returning ships brought back the local cats seen in these far away places — especially if such felines were in any way unusual.

The result of this feline movement meant that in Britain and mainland Europe there existed a growing genetic pool from which most of today's cat breeds have developed. There were large and small cats, short- and longhaired cats, cats without tails, and many cats displaying a range of colors and coat pattern

As the 19th century got underway, there was a growing interest throughout Europe and America about all manner of animals. Not surprisingly, it was only a question of time before cats would become the source of a more specialized group of devotees than those who merely loved and kept them as pets. The singular event, more than any other, that sparked the cat fancy was a cat show held at the Crystal

The beautiful appearance of the Abyssinian's coat is created by the ticking: the dark- and light-colored bands on the hair shafts.

types. Included in these were ticked cats from Russia, Asia, Spain, and the Near East, including Egypt, Libya, the Sudan, and Abyssinia. But this various assemblage comprised no true breeds, only sorts of cats — general types that were given a multitude of local names with the passing centuries.

Palace in Sydenham, London on Thursday, July 13th, 1871. It was organized by Harrison Weir, a fellow of the Horticultural Society and a great lover of cats. The show was an unprecedented success. As a consequence, more shows were organized in Britain, then in Europe and the USA. And so, the cat fancy was born.

## THE EARLY DAYS OF THE ABYSSINIAN

Against the backdrop of shows, the desire to develop breeds was a logical progression and very popular in those days, much as it remains today. It must also be appreciated that those who entered cat shows were not the everyday working people, rather members of the middle and upper classes. They did not want their cats to be of the ordinary street variety, but felines of some status that stood apart from your average "moggy." There was indeed a strong element of snobbery surrounding the cat fancy.

Exactly when and who hit on the idea of developing a breed to be called an Abyssinian seems to have been lost in history. What we know is that in 1868, a Captain Barrett Lennard returned from the British military expedition in Abyssinia (now Ethiopia) with a female cat named Zulu. Although this feline obviously attracted the attention of cat fanciers, she apparently bore little resemblance to the present day breed, other than that she sported a ruddy, red-brown ticked coat, which was considered unusual at that time.

She appears not to have made any contribution to the breed's formation (at least from the documented standpoint) and may have been one of many such cats that came from the Abyssinian area with returning servicemen. What Zulu may have done was to implant the concept for a breed, and the name Abyssinian would have been logical, given where

**All cat owners should be mindful that some varieties of houseplants can be poisonous. Exercise caution in this regard.**

**This Aby kitten is totally oblivious to his feathered friend.**

Zulu was brought from. This would give the breed the benefit of connotations to the cats of the pharaohs.

Harrison Weir and Louis Wain (the first president of the National Cat Society of England) both stated that the developing breed should, more appropriately, be called Abyssinian "type" because

many similar cats existed in Britain at that time. These were bred from litters of domestic shorthairs. Weir is also on record describing the breed as being Russian and Spanish.

In 1882, the Abyssinian was first recognized as a separate breed, but by the time the National Cat Society was founded

The Abyssinian is a lithe, hard, and muscular breed of cat. Owner, Nicole Ledoux.

in 1887, the name was dropped. The breed was variously called the British Ticked, Bunny, or Hare cat. Each of these were thought to better convey the idea of an agouti-marked feline, though they hardly projected any aura of majesty at a time when it was very fashionable to do so. Not until the Abyssinian Cat Club was formed in England during 1919 was the name Abyssinian reinstated and accepted by one and all in the fancy.

During these early days, the Abyssinian was not always the lithe, distinctive, and semi-foreign-looking breed type we know today. Any feline that displayed a ticked coat would qualify as an Abyssinian. The now famous ruddy color was also not preeminent. Many of the cats were silver ticked, which is apparent from their names. Silver was the most fashionable of colors in tabbies during this period.

To give you a sense of their value during the early years of the breed, it is interesting to note that in 1912 a pair of Abyssinians were selling for more than the average worker earned in two months.

### BREED REGISTRATIONS

The first Abyssinians were registered with the National Cat Club in 1896. This can be said to mark the end of the "type" era and beginnings of true breeds. The cats were Sedgemere Bottle, bred in 1892, and Sedgemere Peaty, born in 1894, both from unknown parents and bred by a Mr. Swinyard (the term "unknown"

does not mean the parents were unknown or that they were not Abyssinians, merely that they did not have pedigrees).

A number of Abys entered in the first stud books had one or both parents of unknown ancestry. The creation of a breed, unless it is based on a specific mutation, does not happen overnight. Many of the early breeders did not maintain pedigrees. One can say that, other than being ticked, an Abyssinian was defined as such because its breeders said it was! Only with the passage of time, more registrations, more shows, and the recording of lineages via pedigrees did the breed move away from pragmatic definition to the provable.

It must also be appreciated that during the formative years in any breed there is always an element of disagreement between breeders as to what constitutes the "true" breed. We know that silvers were very popular in the early years. Names such as Aluminum, Platinum, Silver, and Salt would hardly have been applied to ruddy or red (sorrel in the UK) Abys.

As the years passed, the silvers and the yellows lost favor, and the Abyssinian became strongly regarded as being a red-colored cat of varying degrees of intensity. During the 1950s in England, nearly every Abyssinian seen was of the ruddy (usual) color. The breed was still very much a rare breed, strongly associated only with the professional and upper classes.

Abys are mellow, even-tempered cats. Aby fanciers will tell you that they are a delight to own.

Today, things have turned full circle, and depending in which country you live, you can now select from a range of colors that include silver, blue, lilac, chocolate, fawn, cream, and even tortoiseshell. Such colors would undoubtedly have horrified many of the early pioneer breeders whose goal was to create a breed that looked as natural as possible in both its conformation and color pattern. There are still to this day breeders that hold this same view where colors are concerned.

America along with a female called Salt, which was born one month later. She was sired by Aluminum but out of Abeba. This pair are believed to have been the first Abyssinians to arrive in the United States and certainly were from a recorded standpoint.

In the years after this initial import, there are no records of British Abyssinians being registered in the US until 1933. Thereafter, the flow of imports from England was slow but steady as the breed gained limited

Ruddy Aby. In this and all the other color varieties, the ticking should be distinct and even. Owner, Sheila Dentico.

## CROSSING THE ATLANTIC

In 1905, Miss Carew-Cox, one of Britain's most preeminent breeders, bred a male kitten called Aluminum. He proved to be one of the breed's most prolific sires. Many now famous lines trace back to him. In 1907, one of his matings was to Fancy Free, a quality silver Aby also owned by Carew-Cox. Aluminum II was in the resulting litter. This male was exported to Miss J. R. Cathcart in

popularity as a very special feline. However, World War II had a catastrophic effect on the Abyssinian population in Britain. This slowed down the breed's development in the US. However, the seeds had been planted.

In the years following 1945, many superb British Abyssinians arrived in America to augment the small existing genetic pool. This formed the nucleus from which many outstanding champions and

Every Abyssinian possesses a personality all its own. Owner, Meredith Gowell.

quickly saw the potential in the breed. It has won just about every top award in all countries where it is well established. Today, the Abyssinian is one of most popular breeds in both the United States and Britain. It does not begin to rival the enormous following of the Persian, Siamese, or Burmese but is well ahead of most others. There is considerable merit in the fact that it is popular without being an enormous breed in numbers. Immense popularity invariably goes hand in hand with breed regression in one form or another. It is a negative consequence. So far, this has not happened in the Abyssinian. It remains a classic example of and

Owning two Abys is hardly any more work than owning just one. If you decide to get a pair of Abys, they will be good company for each other. Owner, Meredith Gowell.

grand champions were to be bred. The Abyssinian was to remain the choice of true feline connoisseurs until relatively recent times when media projections, such as the Disney movie *The Cat From Outer Space* and the T.F.H. book *This is the Abyssinian Cat* brought the breed to the attention of a much wider audience than the more restrictive world of the show cat.

However, cat shows became larger and more glamorous. They projected the Abyssinian to an even wider breeder audience that testimony to how breeders can take a genetic type, in this case a coat pattern, and with vision, mold it into a breed that looks regal yet natural. So natural, in fact, that it can easily convince an owner that it was indeed a very special cat — the sort befitting a pharaoh of a bygone civilization. A cat that somehow, through divine providence, has survived countless trials and tribulations to weave its special charm around its dedicated followers through the passing ages.

## ABYSSINIAN CONFORMATION

To this point we have concentrated on the coat pattern of the Aby. But equally important to the breed is its conformation. This is lithe and of foreign type as compared to the more cobby build of the domestic shorthairs of Europe and the US. The foreign type was present from the first cat show in the form of a pair of Siamese.

However, in some breeds it has changed dramatically from the early years of this century. The

**Abyssinians are eagerly active cats with a lively interest in their surroundings.**

It will be a while longer before the coat color of these Aby youngsters is fully developed. Abyssinians come in four colors: ruddy, red, blue, and fawn.

# ABYSSINIAN CHARACTER

Domestic cats have a general personality that is shared by any member of the cat family. These are inherent traits that the process of evolution imprinted on them — they make a cat what it is. However, not all cats will display all characteristics to the same degree; each is an individual unto itself.

The same is true of canine breeds. Each is the result of the same selection process that went into molding a group of cats into a very distinctive breed. In doing so, the breed's character was also shaped. The character of a sheepdog is very different than that of a gundog and that, in turn, of a guarding breed. While it cannot be said that cat breeds display such an extensive and distinctive range of breed-related traits as dogs, they nonetheless have them.

The Persian is very different from the Siamese, which is different from the Abyssinian. Breed-related characteristics may

The dark facial markings on this Aby kitten are already quite pronounced.

at times be very subtle, but they are there, as any cat lover who has owned numerous breeds will confirm. Characteristics are also subjective traits — we all see within our cats features and emotions that we believe to be very special, because only by constant and loving interaction between owners and their cats will personalities be fully displayed.

**AN AFFECTIONATE BREED**

The Abyssinian is a breed that craves affection from its owner, yet it can be aloof and independent. It must be given time to itself when it wants it. It is not a breed that should be subjected to the rough handling of children. It is much more an adult's sort of cat. While it will make a fine family feline, it must be said that it is probably at its best in homes where there is no competition for the favors of its owner. It can be a possessive cat and does not readily give its affection unless it has been earned.

When selecting toys for your Aby, choose those that are sturdy and well constructed. Pet shops stock a wide variety of toys that your pet will enjoy.

## INTELLIGENCE & EXERCISE

The Aby is a very intelligent breed, so you must provide it with the opportunity to utilize this faculty. This is done through playful interaction with it. Obtain safe toys from your local pet shop. Balls on a string and cat climbing frames are the sort of toys that enable your Abyssinian to focus its mind on something. These will also enable it to burn up a few calories.

Exercise is important in such an active breed, and an Aby must be allowed to exercise as often as possible. It is a very athletic breed, as its conformation clearly suggests. If on one of its mad dashes from one room to another it destroys a few ornaments, it is a small price to pay for being an owner to such an imperial feline. To an Aby, the world and its owner's home are its oyster. You should keep this very much in mind. Such a noble breed should not be expected to behave like any common street cat, after all it was carefully bred to be a cat of high standard.

The more space you have the better. An Abyssinian will not appreciate restrictions. It will be at its best in a home where it can explore and run around. A home where it enjoys lots of interaction with its human companions.

By all means hang on to your day job, but you must be prepared to devote as much of your spare time as possible to entertaining an Abyssinian. This will result in the full development of its personality. They really do thrive on affection and are unsuited to homes where their owners cannot devote at least some time during each day to handling them.

## THE ULTIMATE KITTEN-CAT

Another trait of most Abyssinians is that they are very much kitten-cats. This means that while many felines become more mature and adult in their demeanor as they grow up, the Aby retains a Peter Pan quality to its personality. It matures physically and emotionally but never loses the mischievous side of its nature it displayed when it was a cute kitty. Always inquisitive and ready for a game, an Aby is only as old as it feels, and it always feels young at heart.

The down side of this characteristic is that to an Aby, curtains and shelves are things for their sole amusement! However, with a bit of training, an Aby is intelligent enough to compromise. It will accept that you must be allowed a few concessions if you are to provide all the other good things in life that such a breed expects,

befitting its status in the social hierarchy of the feline world.

## ELEGANCE

You do not need to be blessed with the flowing coat of a Persian or the bright parti-colors of some breeds to be instantly stamped with that quality we call elegance. The Abyssinian is a true blue-blood, developed by the aristocracy for their own pleasure. Times may have changed, but the regal bearing and majestic look of the Aby oozes superiority without the need to rely on any effects other than those that are inherent within the breed.

It is one of the least exaggerated cats. You cannot point to any particular anatomical feature that is striking. It is the intrinsic way in which all its features combine to say, "Now there is a truly magnificent feline." It is this fact that is, perhaps, the very quintessence of what a natural, yet noble feline is all about.

There are, of course, those who would say that the Abyssinian is a plain-looking breed. But the connoisseur would answer by saying that only when you have tried the lesser wines can you appreciate the quality and refinement of one that has been carefully tended and matured to give of its fragrance and delicate taste. To some, the Aby instantly strikes them as a very special breed. To others, it takes time and experience with other breeds before they can appreciate a feline so gracefully put together in every way.

## A HARDY BREED

For all its regal bearing, the Abyssinian is no pampered lap cat. The breed was developed to be as natural as possible to acquire all the traits needed to live within the homes of humans, but to retain the tough character of its wild forbears. It is not associated with any weakness in its disposition or physical make-up, nor is it subject to the genetic problems evident in some breeds.

Not prone to illness if cared for correctly, an Aby is well able to look after itself should any passing street cat start a fight, but hopefully, it will never be faced with a need to resort to such primeval acts of aggression around your home. It will use its superior intellect and athletic ability to avoid such confrontations.

## THE SENSITIVE ABY

Being such an intelligent breed, Abys can display considerable sensitivity to the moods of their human companions. They are playful when you are in the same spirit, but quiet and affectionate when you are feeling more soulful. This same sensitivity makes for a very alert cat, one that quickly picks up on any unusual noises or the sounds of people approaching their domain — your home. All cats have this faculty that has been retained from the wild to a very high degree in this breed.

The Abyssinian is a breed that, even today, will appeal mostly to those who appreciate subtle fineness in a cat. A quiet sophistication that was envisaged so many years ago became a reality. If you prefer silk to wool or champagne to beer, you will find no better feline than the Abyssinian.

**Your Aby will doubtlessly have a number of favorite spots in your home to which it can retreat when it wants to be alone.**

# THE ABYSSINIAN STANDARD & COLORS

In order to determine the relative quality of an Abyssinian cat, or any other feline, there must be a standard against which the individual can be compared. The standards are prepared by a panel of experts within each cat registration body. Periodically these descriptive documents are amended to take account of progress within the breed, or to place more emphasis on a given aspect that may be regressing. The standard can never be precise, so is open to interpretation.

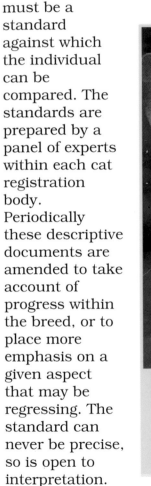

The Abyssinian's eyes, which can be gold or green in color, are accentuated by a fine dark line, encircled by a light-colored area. Ch. Alexys Peggy Sue of Elfin Abys, owned by Denise Ogle-Donahue and Kent Fleming.

Within each standard, points are allocated to various features based on their believed importance within the breed. Any person who has aspirations to exhibit, judge, or breed Abyssinians should have a knowledge of the standard. Only by constantly referring to it can a mental picture be developed of an outstanding Abyssinian.

To the beginner, almost any Abyssinian would seem to be a fine example when he compares it to the standard. The interpretation of the standard becomes meaningful only when combined with the experience of viewing poor, through mediocre, to those adjudged to be outstanding examples of the breed.

## THE ABYSSINIAN STANDARD

The standard quoted in this text is that of the Cat Fanciers Association of America (CFA) and is reproduced by courtesy of that association. The CFA is the largest registration organization in the US and the one most Americans will join.

In Great Britain, there are only two registration bodies and of them the Governing Council of the Cat Fancy (GCCF) is easily the most important, and is also the oldest registry in the world.

If you plan to breed Abyssinians, you are strongly recommended to do so only with registered individuals. You should obtain the show

Abyssinian is lithe, hard and muscular, showing eager activity and a lively interest in all surroundings. Well balanced temperamentally and physically with all elements of the cat in proportion.

*Head:* a modified, slightly rounded wedge without flat planes; the brow, cheek, and profile lines all showing a gentle

**Eight-week-old litter of ruddy Aby kittens. Owner, Judith and Cathy Stanton.**

standards for the registry you plan to support. The standards are not reproduced individually but within booklets that cover all breeds recognized by the registry in question.

*General:* the overall impression of the ideal Abyssinian would be a colorful cat with a distinctly ticked coat, medium in size and regal in appearance. The

contour. A slight rise from the bridge of the nose to the forehead, which should be of good size, with width between the ears and flowing into the arched neck without a break.

*Muzzle:* not sharply pointed or square. The chin should be neither receding nor protruding. Allowance should be made for jowls in adult males.

**Ears:** Alert, large, and moderately pointed; broad and cupped at the base, and set as though listening.

**Eyes:** Almond shaped, large, brilliant, and expressive. Neither round nor oriental.

**Head:** A modified, slightly rounded wedge without flat planes; the brow, cheek, and profile lines all showing a gentle contour.

**Body:** Abyssinian conformation strikes a medium between the extremes of the cobby and the svelte, lengthy type.

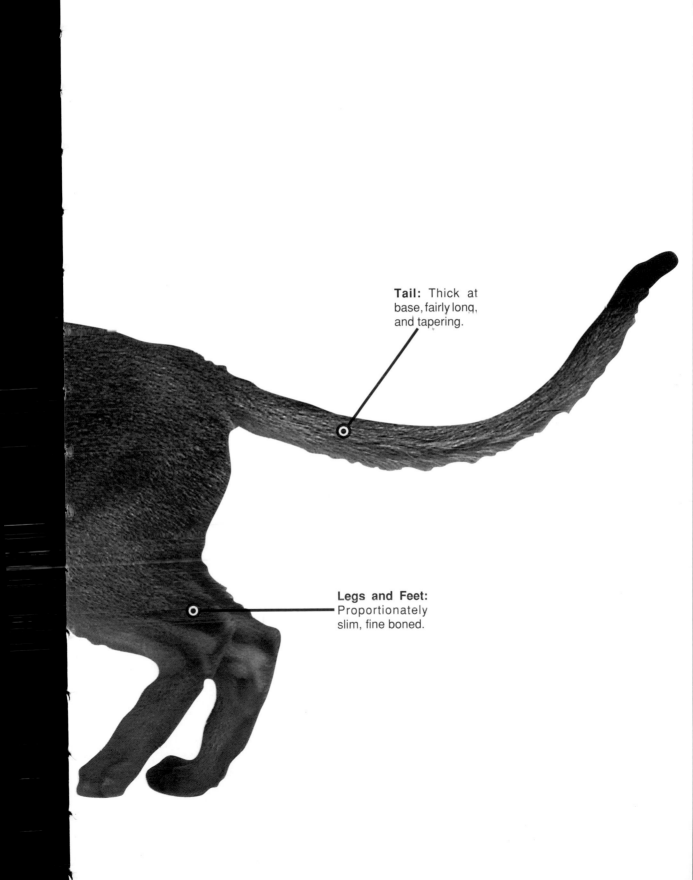

**Tail:** Thick at base, fairly long, and tapering.

**Legs and Feet:** Proportionately slim, fine boned.

*Ears:* alert, large, and moderately pointed; broad, cupped at base, and set as though listening. Hair on ears is very short and close lying, preferably tipped with black or dark brown on a ruddy Abyssinian, chocolate-brown on a red Abyssinian, slate blue on a blue Abyssinian, or light cocoa brown on a fawn Abyssinian.

*Eyes:* almond shaped, large, brilliant, and expressive. Neither round nor oriental. Eyes accentuated by fine dark line, encircled by light-colored area.

*Body:* medium long, lithe, and graceful, but showing well developed muscular strength without coarseness. Abyssinian conformation strikes a medium between the extremes of the cobby and the svelte lengthy type. Proportion and general balance more to be desired than mere size.

*Legs and Feet:* proportionally slim, fine boned. The Abyssinian stands well off the ground giving

**A red Aby's coat will be ticked with chocolate brown, dark at the tips fading to a red undercoat. Owners, Tord and Suzanne Svenson.**

the impression of being on tip toe. Paws small, oval, and compact. Toes: five in front and four behind.

*Tail:* thick at base, fairly long and tapering.

*Coat:* soft, silky, fine in texture, but dense and resilient to the touch with a lustrous sheen. Medium in length but long enough to accommodate two or three dark bands of ticking.

*Penalize:* off-color pads. Long narrow head, short round head. Barring on legs, dark broken necklace markings, rings on tail. Coldness or gray tones in the coat.

*Disqualify:* white locket, or white anywhere other than nostril, chin, and upper-throat area. Kinked or abnormal tail. Dark unbroken necklace. Gray undercoat close to skin extending throughout a major portion of the body. Any black hair on a red Abyssinian. Incorrect number of toes. Any color other than the four accepted colors.

The ruddy (burnt-sienna) Abyssinian has an undercoat that is orange-brown, which fades to black at the tips. Its tail is tipped with black.

## Abyssinian Colors

*Coat color:* warm and glowing. *Ticking:* distinct and even, with dark-colored bands contrasting with lighter-colored bands on the hair shafts. Undercoat color clear and bright to the skin. Deeper color shades desired, however intensity of ticking not to be sacrificed for depth of color. Darker shading along spine allowed if fully ticked. Preference given to cats UNMARKED on the undersides, chest, and legs; tail without rings. *Facial markings:* dark lines extending from the eyes and brows, cheek bone shading, dots and shading on the whisker pads are all desired enhancements. Eyes accentuated by fine dark line, encircled by light-colored area. *Eye color:* gold or green, the more richness and depth of color the better.

*Ruddy:* coat ruddy brown (burnt-sienna), ticked with various shades of darker brown or black; the extreme outer tip to be the darkest, with orange-brown undercoat. Tail tipped with black. The underside and inside of legs to be a tint that harmonizes with the main color. The *nose leather* is tile red. The *paw pads* are black or brown, with black between the toes, extending slightly beyond the paws.

*Red:* coat rich, warm, glowing red, ticked with chocolate brown, the extreme outer tip to be dark, with red undercoat. Tail tipped with chocolate brown. The underside and inside of legs to be a tint that harmonizes with the main color. The *nose leather* is rosy pink. The *paw pads* are pink with chocolate brown between the toes, extending slightly beyond the paws.

*Blue:* coat warm beige, ticked with various shades of slate blue, the extreme outer tip to be darkest, with blush beige undercoat. Tail tipped with slate blue. The underside and inside of legs to be a tint that

Fawn Abyssinians have a warm rose beige coat ticked with light cocoa brown. Owner, Gail Christie.

Blue Abyssinians have a warm-beige coat ticked with various shades of slate blue, the extreme outer tip to be the darkest, with blush beige undercoat.

harmonizes with the main color. The *nose leather* is old rose. The *paw pads* are mauve with slate blue between the toes, extending slightly beyond the paws.

*Fawn:* coat warm rose-beige, ticked with light cocoa brown, the extreme outer tip to be the darkest, with blush beige undercoat. Tail tipped with light cocoa brown. The underside and inside of the legs to be a tint that harmonizes with the main color. The *nose leather* is salmon. The *paw pads* are pink with light cocoa brown between the toes, extending slightly beyond the paws.

**Point Score of the CFA**

| | |
|---|---|
| *Head* | (35) |
| Muzzle | 6 |
| Skull | 6 |
| Ears | 7 |
| Eye shape | 6 |
| *Body* | (30) |
| Torso | 15 |
| Legs and feet | 10 |
| Tail | 5 |
| *Coat* | (10) |
| Texture | 10 |
| *Color* | (30) |
| Color | 15 |
| Ticking | 15 |
| Eye color | 5 |

*There are no allowable outcrosses in the Abyssinan breed.*

# SELECTING AN ABYSSINIAN CAT

**THE QUALITY OF YOUR PET**

Abyssinians come in a range of qualities from the inferior, through the typical examples of the breed, to those which are show winners, or at least potentially so. You may wish to own a high-quality Abyssinian even though you have no intention to show it. Quality means it will have good bone conformation, the correct stature, and its color or patterns will be of a high standard. Such a cat will be a costly purchase. A typical Abyssinian will be just that. It will display no glaring faults and its color will be sound. It may display some minor failings in type or color that would preclude it from ever being of show quality.

An inferior Abyssinian will be one which has obvious faults, either its conformation, its coat quality, poor color or in other ways inferior. Such cats are often described as being pet quality. As long as you appreciate that this term means inferior, its use is fine. However, there are two kinds of inferior Abyssinians. There is the cat which is inferior only in respect to its type and color—not in relation to its basic structure and health.

There is then the inferior cat produced by those who are in Abyssinians just to make money. These people have cats that they breed with no consideration for the vigor of the offspring. Such kittens are invariably sickly and

Kittens should spend at least their first eight weeks of life with their mother. This will help to ensure that they grow into healthy, strong adult cats.

Play fighting is a normal part of Aby kitten behavior. Owner, Judith and Cathy Stanton.

You can provide your cat with its own entertainment center...include a scratching post and things that it likes to play with.

prone to illnesses throughout their lives. Poor health and inferior Abyssinians result from unplanned matings and excessive breeding, coupled with a lack of ongoing selection being applied to future breeding stock.

How do you make the right choice when selecting an Abyssinian? The answer is you do your homework. Visit shows, talk to established exhibitors, and judges. When you visit the seller take a good look at his stock, and more especially the living conditions of the cats. Is he giving you the hard sell, or does he seem more concerned about the kitten's future home? Sometimes the dedicated seller might even annoy you, but he is concerned for his kittens, even if they are not quality Abyssinians. The more Abyssinians you see, the more likely you are to make a wise choice.

## WHICH SEX TO PURCHASE?

From the viewpoint of pet suitability, there really is no difference between a tom (male) and a queen (female). Some people prefer one sex, but this is purely subjective. This author has found males to be more consistent in their character than females, who may tend to be "all or nothing" in their attitude. In other words, they can be extremely affectionate one day, but rather standoffish the next. The tom tends to be much the same from one day to the next, whatever his character might be.

It really is a pot-luck matter just how affectionate a kitten will grow up to become. Cats are very much individuals, and they can change as they grow up. The way they are treated also affects their personality. Therefore, it is more a case of selecting a kitten that appeals to you, regardless of its sex.

Of course, if you wish to become a breeder then the female has to be the better choice. Once she reaches breeding age you can then select a suitable mate for her from the hundreds of quality stud males available to you. If you purchase a male with the view to owning a stud, you are really gambling that he will mature into a fine cat that others would want to use. For this to happen, your tom would need to be very successful in the show ring, and then in the quality of his offspring.

Furthermore, owning a whole tom (a male that has not been neutered) does present more practical problems than owning a queen. Such a male will be continually marking his territory (your furniture) by spraying it with his urine, which is hardly a fragrant scent!

If your Abyssinian is to be a pet only, then regardless of the sex you should have it neutered or spayed. It will be more affectionate to you, will not be wandering off looking for romance, and will not shed its coat as excessively as would an unaltered Abyssinian. In the case of a tom, he will not come home with pieces of his ears missing as a result of his fights with other entire males. Your queen will not present you with kittens that you do not want but which she will have if she is not spayed. She is far less likely to spray than is the male, but she will show her desire to mate, both with her "calling" sounds, which can be eerie, and her provocative crouching position in which she is clearly inviting a mating.

## WHAT AGE TO PURCHASE?

Breeders vary in the age they judge a kitten ready for a new home. An important consideration is obviously if the new owners have experience of cats generally and kittens in particular. While an eight-week-old baby is quite delightful, it is invariably better from a health standpoint that the kitten remains with its mother until it is ten or more weeks of age. Some breeders will not part with a kitten until it is 16 weeks of age.

**Your Aby will appreciate a soft, comfortable place in which it can rest and sleep.**

The kitten should have received at least temporary vaccinations against feline distemper and rabies (if applicable in your country and if the kitten is over 12 weeks of age) and preferably protection against other major feline infections. Additionally, you should let your own vet examine your Abyssinian.

Although most owners will wish to obtain a kitten, a potential breeder or exhibitor may find that a young adult (over eight to nine months of age) is more suitable to his needs. By this age the quality of the Abyssinian is becoming more apparent. However, bear in mind that a mature Abyssinian queen will not be at her peak until she is about two years of age. A tom will be even later in reaching full maturity, and he may not peak until he is five years of age.

## ONE OR TWO ABYSSINIANS?

Without any doubt, two kittens are always preferred to one. They provide constant company for each other and are a delight to watch as they play. The extra costs involved in their upkeep are unlikely to be a factor if you are able to afford an Abyssinian in the first place.

# GENERAL CARE & GROOMING

Abyssinian cats are extremely easy to cater to in terms of their accommodations and general care. This chapter will discuss purchasing the essential and nonessential accessories for your cat, socializing your cat with children and other animals, making a safe environment for your cat, and disciplining your cat the proper and most effective way.

## ABSOLUTE ESSENTIALS

While keeping a cat is essentially a simple task, there are certain items that the cat owner absolutely must have if he expects to keep his kitty happy and well. The following items should be purchased from your local pet store or supply center before you bring the cat into your home. Don't try to find bargains! Buy the best the first time and you won't have to replace it as often. Pet shops offer the finest pet supplies, the propietors will be happy to advise you which is the most effective and best for your particular cat.

This Abyssinian kitten displays the sweet, wide-eyed expression typical of its breed.

## Litter Tray

Every cat will need a litter tray so that it can relieve itself whenever it wishes to. If this is not provided from the outset, the only possible consequence is that the cat will be forced to foul your carpet or some other surface. There are many styles and sizes of litter trays, and the larger ones are the best for long-term service. Some have igloo-type hoods, both to provide a sense of privacy for the cat and to retain any odors. However, an open tray is just as good and will not in any case be foul smelling if it is cleaned as it should be.

You will need to purchase cat litter for the base of the tray. There are many brands to choose from, and some have odor neutralizers already in them. Cover the base with enough litter to absorb urine and for the cat to scratch around in. In the event you should run out of litter, you can use coarse grade sawdust or wood shavings. These are preferred to

A cat carrier is one of the most important purchases that you will make for your Abyssinian. It will enable you to transport your pet safely and comfortably.

garden soil because the latter may contain the eggs of parasitic worms or other parasites.

The tray should be cleaned after each use, removing that which is soiled. A small dustpan is handy for attending to this chore. Once a week, you should disinfect and thoroughly rinse the tray.

Housetraining is easily accomplished with a kitten. When you see it searching for somewhere to relieve itself, which will be accompanied by crying, it should be gently lifted and placed into its tray. Never scold a kitten for fouling the floor, it will not understand why you are annoyed with it. You must watch the kitten after it has played and after it wakes up because these are prime times for it to want to relieve itself. Remember, kittens cannot control their bowel movements for more than a few seconds; this time increases considerably as the cat matures. If you exhibit patience, you will find the kitty quickly gets to know what is expected of it. Cats are fastidious about cleanliness, so if they foul the home, there is invariably a reason for so doing. Often it will be because the litter tray has not been cleaned or you were not around enough when the cat was a kitten.

## Scratching Post

Here again, there are many styles to choose from. All have a fabric on them, and the post may be free standing or the sort that is screwed to a wall. You can also purchase carpet-clad climbing frames, which are more expensive but greatly enjoyed by cats. When you see your kitten or cat go to scratch your armchair, lift it up and place it against the scratching post. Gently draw its front feet down the post a few times. Again, if this is repeated a number of times, the kitten will understand that it can claw away on the post but not on the furniture. As it grows older, it will no doubt test your resolve now and then, but usually if you clap your hands and say "No" in a firm voice, it will realize you are keeping an eye on it!

Scratching posts offer hours of healthy exercise and enjoyment for cats and kittens while preventing them from damaging the furniture. Photo courtesy of Cosmic Pet Products.

## Cat Collar

All cats should wear a cat collar fitted with an ID tag. In many cities, this is a law. An elastic collar wil prevent the possiblility of its getting snagged, thus possibly choking the cat. Be sure it is neither too tight nor too loose. You should be able to place a finger between the collar and the cat's neck.

### Carry Box

The carry box is so useful that I regard it as an essential item for all cat owners. It will be needed when you visit the vet, when traveling, or when you need to contain the cat for any reason. It also makes a fine bed for a kitten. The box can be made of wicker, wood, wire, or fiberglass. The latter are probably the best but can be companion. If not, place a cuddly toy in with it to snuggle up against. When it is a kitten and during its first week or so in its new home, it is better that it is confined at night, so it cannot harm itself by wandering about the home. Once it is totally familiar with your home, you can leave the carry-box door open at night so it can come and go as it wishes.

Select a litter box that is sturdy and easy to clean. Change the litter regularly : cats will not tolerate an overly dirty litter box; and if they are forced to do so, they may choose to attend to their toilet needs elsewhere.

expensive if they are of a high quality. It is essential that they should be large enough for the adult cat to stand upright in and not be forced to stoop.

The base of the box can be fitted with a good lining of newspaper on which a blanket is placed. A kitten will find this a nice bed, especially if it has a

### Feeding Dishes

You will want one dish for moist cat food, one for dry food, and one for water. You can purchase dishes made of earthenware, aluminum, stainless steel, or plastic. You can also use saucers or any combination of these. The main thing is that they are kept spotlessly clean, so they should

**This Aby is thoroughly content in the company of her canine companion. Cats and dogs can get along well if they are introduced at a young age.**

be washed after each use. The water dish should be cleaned and replenished each day.

**Brush**

Cats do not come any simpler to groom than an Abyssinian. Even so, your cat should have its own brush, preferably of a medium-bristle type. A chamois leather or silk cloth is also useful to give your cat that extra sheen after it has been brushed. Although the Abyssinian hardly needs any brushing, it is useful to attend to this once a week. This makes your cat familiar with being handled, and at such a time, you can give it a check over. Inspect its ears to see that they are free of wax and check the teeth to see that they are

clean. Inspect the pads to ensure that they are firm but supple. Part the toes with your fingers just to make sure they are free of debris. Lodged in the skin, dirt and grass could be the source of an abscess if they are not removed. Gently feel the abdomen to check that there are no swellings.

**BEYOND THE BASICS**

Pet lovers love to lavish their pet with all kinds of goodies, and for a cat owner, the sky is the limit when it comes to choosing special accessories for his pet. The ever-expanding pet industry makes it easy for cat owners to find new and inventive ways to entertain and better care for their feline friends.

Abyssinians are active and agile. These two youngsters are perfecting their balancing act.

The exotic beauty of the Abyssinian sets it apart from many of the other breeds of cat.

**Basket or Bed**

If you obtain a carry box for your kitten, then a bed is not a necessity.  Cats like to choose their own place to sleep, and indeed they will have numerous places depending on their mood, the ambient temperature, and who happens to be in your home at a given time. Some will have a favorite chair or sofa, some may prefer a secluded spot behind a chair, while others will prefer to sleep on your bed, knowing this to be a warm and popular place with their "human-cat" companions.

Better than a conventional basket would be to invest in one of the many carpet-clad, wooden furniture pieces produced these days for cats. These are fun and take into account the cat's preference for sleeping above floor level. Some cats do sleep in baskets, so it is a case of reviewing all the options and deciding which you think will best meet your needs.

**Halter or Harness**

If you plan on taking your cat with you on vacation or generally when you travel, it will be found that a cat collar does not offer you full control over your Abyssinian. Additionally to the collar, you could purchase one of the numerous halters now available for cats. Choose one that fits snugly. Those with top fastenings are easy to place on your cat. Do not obtain dog harnesses because they will be too big around the chest, even if they are for small dogs.

Lead training is best done while your pet is young. Place the halter on the kitten and let it become familiar with it before you attempt to attach the lead. When the halter does not bother the cat, you can then attach the lead and let the cat wander about in the privacy of your yard. Here it will become used to the fact that there is a restraint on its movements. The process cannot be hurried because cats do not like to be restricted. Only devote a few minutes per day to lead training and always encourage the cat with a treat.

Do not take the cat from the confines of its home territory until it is really relaxed on a lead. In the event of a dog suddenly appearing, the halter allows you to maintain control of the cat, which should be promptly lifted up. If it is not your intention to take your cat on regular outings, there is little point in lead training it because cats are generally not happy away from their home range.

**Toys**

There is no shortage of commercially made cat toys these days. Avoid soft, plastic ones that your pet might break apart and swallow pieces from. If you devote time to playing with your cats, you will find that they will learn how to play games with you, and it will strengthen the bond between you and your cat.

**CATS AND CHILDREN**

If there are young children in your home, it is most important that they are taught from the outset to respect your new kitten or cat. Children must understand that cats should not be disturbed if they are sleeping and should not be handled in an incorrect manner. When being lifted, a cat should never be grasped by the loose fur on its neck. Always support the full body weight with one hand, while securing the cat firmly but gently around the neck with the other hand.

Children should be made aware of the fact that even kittens can inflict a nasty scratch on them if the kitten is not treated with kindness and consideration. Essentially, you must always be watchful if young children are playing with the family cat until they are old enough to understand how it must be handled.

## CATS AND OTHER PETS

The cat is a prime predator and should not be left in the company of young rabbits, guinea pigs, hamsters, or mice if these other pets are out of their cage. As a general rule, if a pet is as big as your cat or is another carnivore, it will usually be safe. Cats and dogs get on really well if they are brought up together. However, if a kitten is introduced into a home that has an adult dog, due care must be exercised. The first thing to ensure is that the resident pet gets extra attention so it does not become jealous of the new arrival.

The kitten and other pets must come to terms with each other in their own time and manner — it is not something you can hurry. In some instances, a newly acquired cat may make friends very quickly with dogs or other household

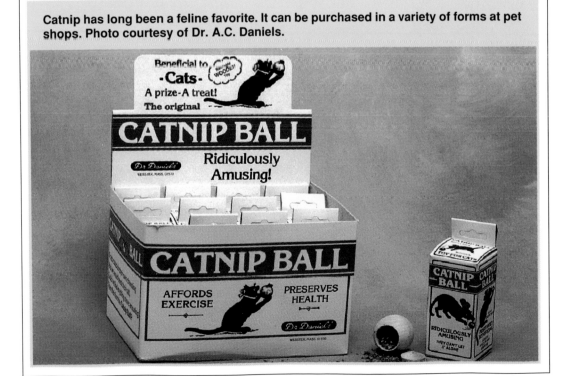

Catnip has long been a feline favorite. It can be purchased in a variety of forms at pet shops. Photo courtesy of Dr. A.C. Daniels.

Good grooming habits should start at an early age. Your pet shop can help you to select the proper grooming aids for your cat. Photo courtesy of The Kong Company.

open fire is yet another example of how a kitten might easily become injured. They are, of course, naturally cautious of dangerous situations, but even so, it is best to watch out for them just as their mother would.

The kitchen is probably the most dangerous place for kittens. A typical scenario is that you might turn around from the stove with a pan of boiling water or a kettle in your hand, only to trip over the kitten. The water may scald the kitten or yourself badly, and the fall would not do you any good either! Kittens just love to pounce and hang onto string and its like. The latter might be the cord from an electric iron you are using — the result being obvious. As your Abyssinian

cats. In other cases, the best that ever happens is a sort of truce, each accepting the other but avoiding contact most of the time. Kittens will invariably be accepted much more readily than will adult cats. The latter, of course, will have developed their own attitudes to other animals depending on what their experiences have been with them.

### SAFEGUARDING A KITTEN

When a kitten is first introduced to your home, there are many potential dangers that it must be protected from. For example, a door left ajar on a windy day could easily slam shut on the kitty. An unprotected balcony is an obvious danger to a young feline, as is a garden pond. An

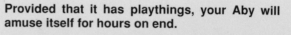

Provided that it has playthings, your Aby will amuse itself for hours on end.

**Take precautions to safeguard your Aby against potential household dangers. Owner, Dean Mastrangelo.**

gets a little older, it will easily be able to jump onto kitchen units and should be educated at an early age not to do this in this particular room.

The other important area of safeguarding a kitten is in relation to ensuring it is given maximum protection against major feline diseases. This is done via vaccinations. Consult your vet about these as soon as you have obtained your Abyssinian. Do not allow the kitten out of the house until it has complete protection.

### DISCIPLINE

Cats are very intelligent and respond to discipline just as dogs and most other comparable pets will. They are not dangerous to people so do not need the level of training that a dog does to fit into a human world. It's really a case in which your cat should understand one simple command—"no." If it goes to scratch the furniture, you should promptly lift it up and say, "No." A very light tap on its rump will enforce the command. This is about the extent of discipline that will ever be needed.

The most important thing you must remember whether training a cat, a dog, a horse, or a large parrot, is that they relate only to the moment. The longer the time lapse between the act and discipline, the less chance there is that the animal will associate one action with another. You can work on the basis that if you are unable to administer discipline within seconds of an unwanted act, you may as well not bother. If the kitten or cat is out of distance, clapping your hands at the same time as saying the command can be effective. Alternatively, you might be able to throw some light object at the cat at the same time as the command is given.

All animal training is based on the fact that the animal associates a given action with a given response. The latter will either be neutral (i.e. nothing happens), positive, or negative. Neither cats nor dogs will understand a lengthy lecture, but they will rapidly understand instant responses to their own actions. You will thus use both positive and negative "enforcers" in training your cat. If your Abyssinian meows for some food or to go out and you respond promptly, this will enforce the action that will be repeated at a later date. The more you respond, the greater will be implantation of that action in the cat. The same goes for discipline.

You should never need to use forcible discipline with a cat. If you think carefully about any given action and apply an appropriate response fairly and consistently (the latter being crucial), you will develop a real understanding with your feline friend.

Crouched low to the ground and moving stealthily, this fawn Aby exhibits the posture typical of a cat whose curiosity has been aroused. Owner, Diane Jackson.

Abyssinians are intelligent, responsive cats. Owner, Meredith Gowell.

other meat bones that still have some meat on them will be enjoyed and keep a kitten or cat amused for quite some time. Beware of bones that easily splinter, such as those of chicken or rabbit.

You can by all means see if small pieces of vegetables or fruits are accepted if mixed with the food, but generally cats will leave them. This is no problem providing that the cat is receiving commercial foods as its basic diet. Such products are all fortified with essential vitamins after the cooking process.

## HOW MUCH TO FEED?

Cats prefer to eat a little but often, rather than consume one mighty meal a day. However, as carnivores, adults are well able to cope with one large meal a day. The same is not true of kittens, which should receive three or four meals per day. A kitten or a cat will normally only consume that which is needed. You can arrive at this amount by trial and error. If kitty devours its meal and is looking for more, then let it have more. You will quickly be able to

Commercial cat foods are available in three varieties: moist, semi moist, and dry, which is what this Aby is fed. Owner, Meredith Gowell.

judge how much each kitten needs to satisfy itself. Always remove any moist foods that are uneaten after each meal.

At 12 weeks of age the kitten should have four meals a day. One of these meals can be omitted when the kitten is 16 weeks old, but increase the quantity of the other three. You can reduce to two meals a day when the kitten is about nine months of age. From that age, it is best to continue feeding two meals—one in the morning and one in the early evening. How many times a day you feed your adult cat is unimportant. The key factor is that it receives as much as it needs over the day, and that the diet is balanced to provide the essential ingredients discussed earlier. It is also better that meals are given regularly. Cats, like humans, are creatures of habit.

## WATER

If a cat's diet is essentially of moist foods, it will drink far less than if the diet is basically of dry foods. Many cats do not like faucet (tap) water because they are able to smell and taste the

Kittens should be fed four times daily. Adult cats can be fed twice a day. Fresh water should be available at all times. Owner, Meredith Gowell.

many additives included by your local water board. Chlorine is high on this list. Although it dissipates into the air quite readily, chloromides do not, which is why the cat may ignore the water. During the filtering process at the water station, chemicals are both taken out and added. The resulting mineral balance and taste is often not to a cat's liking. This is why you will see cats drinking from puddles, a flower vase, or even your toilet, because the taste is better for them. If your water is refused, then you can see if your cat prefers mineralized bottled water—not distilled because the latter has no mineral content to it.

## THE NEW ARRIVAL

It is a very traumatic time for a kitten when it leaves its mother and siblings. It will often eat well the first day; however, as it starts to miss its family, it will fret. You can reduce its stress by providing the diet it was receiving from the seller. You can change the diet slowly, if necessary, as it settles down. Of course, many kittens have no problems, but if yours does, this feeding advice should help its period of adjustment.

What is essential is that the kitten takes in sufficient liquids so that it does not start to dehydrate. This, more than anything else, will adversely affect its health very rapidly. If you are at all concerned, do consult your vet. The kitten may have picked up a virus, but if it is treated promptly, this should not be a problem. Your vet might supply you with a dietary supplement, which we have found excellent for kittens experiencing "new home syndrome."

# YOUR ABYSSINIAN'S HEALTH

Like any other animal, your Abyssinian can fall victim to hundreds of diseases and conditions. Most can be prevented by sound husbandry. The majority, should they be recognized in their early stages, can be treated with modern drugs or by surgery. Clearly, preventive techniques are better and less costly than treatments, yet in many instances a cat will become ill because the owner has neglected some basic aspect of general management. In this chapter, we are not so much concerned with cataloging all the diseases your cat could contract, because these are legion, but more concerned with reviewing sound management methods.

## HYGIENE

Always apply routine hygiene to all aspects of your pet's management. This alone dramatically reduces the chances of your pet becoming ill because it restricts pathogens (disease-causing organisms) from building up colonies that are able to overcome the natural defense mechanisms of your Abyssinian.

Like all other cats, the Abyssinian is a clean animal that is meticulous in its grooming habits. A cat may groom itself several times throughout the day.

1. After your cat has eaten its fill of any moist foods, either discard the food or keep it for later by placing it in your refrigerator. Anything left uneaten at the end of the day can be trashed. Always wash the bowl after each meal. Do not feed your pet from any dishes that are chipped, cracked, or, in the case of plastic, those that are badly scratched.

2. Always store food in a dry, cool cupboard or in the refrigerator in the case of fresh foods.

3. For whatever reason, if you have been handling someone else's cats, always wash your hands before handling your own cats.

4. Be rigorous in cleaning your cat's litter box as soon as you see that it has been fouled.

5. Pay particular attention to the grooming of an Abyssinian cat because so many problems

Some Abys are attracted to water, and their favorite spot in the house is the bathroom sink! Owner, Meredith Gowell.

can begin with a seemingly innocuous event. For example, in itself, a minor cut may not be a major problem as long as it is treated with an antiseptic. But if it is left as an open untreated wound, it is an obvious site for bacterial colonization. The bacteria then gain access to the bloodstream, and a major problem ensues that might not even be associated with the initial wound. The same applies to flea or lice bites. Inspect the skin carefully for signs of flea droppings when you groom an Abyssinian. These appear like minute specks of black dust.

## RECOGNIZING AN ILL CAT

You must be able to recognize when your cat is ill in order to seek a solution to the problem. You must learn to distinguish between a purely temporary condition and that which will need some form of veterinary advice and/or treatment. For example, a cat can sprain a muscle by jumping and landing awkwardly. This would normally correct itself over a 36-48 hour period. Your pet may contract a slight chill, or its feces might become loose. Both conditions will normally correct themselves over a day or so. On the other hand, if a condition persists for more than two days, it would be advisable to telephone your vet for advice.

In general, any appearance or behavior that is not normal for your cat would suggest something is responsible for the abnormality. This is your first indication that something may be amiss. The following are a number of signs that indicate a problem:

1. Diarrhea, especially if it is very liquid, foul-smelling or blood-streaked. If blood is seen in the urine, this is also an indication of a problem, as is excessive straining or cries of pain when the cat tries to relieve itself.

2. Discharge from the nose or eyes. Many Abyssinians may discharge a liquid from the eyes due to blocked tear ducts. This is associated with the foreshortening of the muzzle. However, an excessive discharge needs veterinary attention.

3. Repeated vomiting. All cats are sick occasionally with indigestion. They will also vomit after eating grass, but repeated vomiting is not normal.

4. Wheezing sounds when breathing, or any other suggestion of breathing difficulties.

5. Excessive scratching. All cats will have a good scratch on a quite regular basis, but excessive scratching indicates a skin problem, especially if it has created sores or lesions.

6. Constant rubbing of the rear end along the ground.

7. Bald patches, lesions, cuts, and swellings on the body, legs, tail, or face.

8. The coat seems to lack bounce or life, and is dull.

9. The cat is listless and lethargic, showing little interest in what is going on around it.

10. The eyes have a glazed look to them, or the haw (nictitating membrane, or third eyelid) is clearly visible.

11. The cat is displaying an unusual lack of interest in its favorite food items.

12. The gums of the teeth seem very red or swollen.

13. Fits or other abnormal signs of behavior.

14. Any obvious pain or distress.

Very often two or more clinical signs will be apparent when a condition is developing. The number of signs increases as the disease or ailment advances to a more sinister stage.

**DIAGNOSIS**

Correct diagnosis is of the utmost importance before any form of treatment can be administered. Often it will require blood and/or fecal microscopy in order to establish the exact cause of a condition. Many of the signs listed above are common to most diseases, so never attempt home diagnosis and treatment: if you are wrong, your cherished Abyssinian may pay for your error with its life. Once ill health is suspected, any lost time favors the pathogens and makes treatment both more difficult and more costly.

In making your original decision to purchase an Abyssinian, or any other cat, you should always have allowed for the cost of veterinary treatment. If this is likely to be a burden that you cannot afford, then do not purchase a cat. The first few months, and especially the first weeks, is the time when most cats will become ill. If they survive this period, the chances are that future visits to the vet will be rare, other than for booster vaccinations.

Kittens do not have the immunity to pathogens that the adult cat does, nor do they have the muscle reserves of the adult. If they are ill, they need veterinary help very quickly if they are to have a good chance of overcoming a disease or major problem.

Having decided that your cat is not well, you should make notes on paper of the signs of the problem, when you first noticed them, and how quickly things have deteriorated. If possible, obtain a fecal and urine sample, then telephone your vet and make an appointment. Ask other cat owners in your area who their vet is. Some vets display a greater liking for cats, or dogs, or horses than do others. This is just human nature, but obviously you

This show-quality Aby is the picture of health. Owner, Tord and Suzanne Svenson.

want to go to one that has a special affection for felines.

## TREATMENT

Once your vet has prescribed a course of treatment, it is important that you follow it exactly as instructed. Do not discontinue the medicine because the cat shows a big improvement. Such an action could prove

reduce the risk of them infecting your Abyssinian. The bacteria and viruses that cause such diseases are often found in the air wherever there are cats. Discuss a program of immunization with your vet.

When a kitten is born, it inherits protection from disease via the colostrum of its mother's milk. Such protection may last for

A hungry litter of Abys nursing. During their first few weeks of life, these kittens will get all of the nutrients that they need from their mother's milk.

counterproductive, and the pathogens that had not been killed might develop an immunity to the treatment. A relapse could occur, and this might be more difficult to deal with.

## VACCINATIONS

There are a few extremely dangerous diseases that afflict cats, but fortunately there are vaccines that can dramatically

up to 16 weeks—but it varies from kitten to kitten and may last only six weeks. It is therefore recommended that your kitten be vaccinated against diseases at six to eight weeks of age just to be on the safe side. Boosters are required some weeks later and thereafter each year. Potential breeding females should be given boosters about three to four weeks prior to the due date. This will ensure that a high level of antibodies is passed to the kittens.

An important consideration with regard to the major killer diseases in cats is the treatment of infection. If a cat survives an infection, it will probably be a carrier of the disease and shed the pathogens continually throughout its life. The only safe course is therefore to ensure that your kittens are protected. The main diseases for which there are vaccinations are as follows:

**Rabies:** This is a disease of the neurological system. It is non-existent in Great Britain, Ireland, Australia, New Zealand, Hawaii, certain oceanic islands, Holland, Sweden, and Norway. In these countries, extremely rigid quarantine laws are applied to ensure it stays that way. You cannot have your cat vaccinated against rabies if you live in one of these countries, unless you are about to emigrate with your cat. In all other countries, rabies vaccinations are either compulsory or strongly advised. They are given when the kitten is three or more months of age.

**Feline panleukopenia:** Also known as feline infectious enteritis, and feline distemper. This is a highly contagious viral disease. Vaccinations are given when the kitten is about eight weeks old, and a booster is given four weeks later. In high-risk areas, a third injection may be advised four weeks after the second one.

**Feline respiratory disease complex:** Often referred to as cat flu but this is incorrect. Although a number of diseases are within this group, two of them are especially dangerous. They are feline viral rhinotracheitis (FVR) and feline

Abyssinian litters are smaller than the litters of other cats. Aby litter size ranges from one to three.

calicivirus (FCV). The vaccination for the prevention of these diseases is combined and given when the kitten is six or more weeks of age; a booster follows three to four weeks later.

**Feline leukemia virus complex (FeLV):** This disease was first recognized in 1964, and a vaccine became available in the US in about 1985. Like "cat flu," the name is misleading, because it is far more complex than a blood cancer, which is what its name implies. Essentially, it destroys the cat's immune system, so the cat may contract any of the major diseases.

The disease is easily spread via the saliva of a cat as it licks other cats. It is also spread prenatally from an infected queen to her offspring via the blood, or when washing her kittens. This is why it is important to test all breeding cats for FeLV. Vaccination is worthwhile only on a kitten or cat that has tested negative. If a cat tests positive for the disease, it has a 70 percent chance of survival, though it will be a carrier in many instances.

**Feline infectious peritonitis (FIP):** This disease has various effects on the body's metabolism. There are no satisfactory tests for it, but intranasal liquid vaccinations via a dropper greatly reduce the potential for it to develop in the tissues of the nose.

## PARASITES

Parasites are organisms that live on or in a host. They feed from it without providing any benefit in return. External parasites include fleas, lice, ticks, flies, and any other creature that bites the skin of the cat. Internal parasites include all pathogens, but the term is more commonly applied to worms in their various forms.

External parasites and their eggs can be seen with the naked eye. All can be eradicated with treatment from your vet. However, initial treatment will need to be followed by further treatments because most compounds are ineffective on the eggs. The repeat treatments kill the larvae as they hatch. It is also important that all bedding be treated or destroyed because this is often where parasites prefer to live when not on the host.

All cats are host to a range of worm species. If worms multiply in the cat, they adversely affect its health. They will cause loss of appetite, wasting, and a steady deterioration in health. At a high level of infestation, they may be seen in the fecal matter, but normally it will require fecal microscopy by your vet. This will establish the species and the relative density of the eggs, thus the level of infestation.

Treatment is normally via tablets, but liquids are also available. Because worms are so common, the best husbandry technique is to routinely treat breeding cats for worms prior to their being bred, then for the queen and her kittens to be treated periodically. Discuss a testing and treatment program with your vet.

## NEUTERING AND SPAYING

Desexing your cat is normally done when a female is about four months of age and somewhat later with a male. The operation is quite simple with a male but more complicated with a female. It is still a routine procedure. It is possible to delay estrus in a breeding queen, but the risk of negative side effects makes this a dubious course to take. Discuss it with your vet. A cat of any age can be neutered (male) or spayed (female); but if they are adults, they take some months (especially males) before they lose their old habits.

## FIRST AID

Although you might think that such inquisitive creatures as cats would be prone to many physical injuries, this is not actually the case. They usually extricate themselves from dangerous situations because of their very fast reflexes. However, injuries do happen, and the most common is caused by the cat darting across a road and being hit by a vehicle. About 40 percent of cats die annually due to traffic accidents. The next level of injury will be caused by cats getting bitten or scratched when fighting among themselves, or being bitten by an insect, or by a sharp object getting lodged in their fur or feet.

If your cat is hit by a vehicle, the first thing to do is to try and place it on a board of some sort and remove it to a safe place. Do not lift its head because this might result in it swallowing blood into the lungs. Try to keep it calm by talking soothingly to it.

If the cat is still mobile, but has clearly been badly hurt, you must try and restrict its movements by wrapping it in a blanket or towel. If it is bleeding badly, try to contain the flow by wrapping a bandage around the body or leg to reduce the blood loss. With a minor cut, you should trim the hair away from the wound, bathe it, then apply an antiseptic or stem the flow with a styptic pencil or other coagulant.

If you suspect that your cat has been bitten by an insect and the result is a swelling, the poison is already in the skin so external ointments will have virtually no effect. The same is true of an abscess caused by fighting. The only answer is to let your vet use surgery to lance and treat the wound.

Fortunately, cats rarely swallow poison because they are such careful eaters. In all instances, immediately contact your vet and advise him of the kind of poison the cat has consumed.

If your cat should ever be badly frightened, for example, by a dog chasing and maybe biting it, the effect of this may not be apparent immediately. It may go into shock some time later. Keep the cat indoors so that you can see how it reacts. Should it go into shock and collapse, place a blanket around it and take it to the vet. If this is not possible, place it in a darkened room and cover it with a blanket so it does not lose too much body heat. Comfort it until you can make contact with the vet.

# EXHIBITING ABYSSINIANS

From the first time cats were seriously exhibited in London in 1871, the cat show has been the very heart of the fancy. It is the place where breeders can have the merits of their stock assessed in a competitive framework, where all cat lovers can meet and discuss ideas, trends and needs, and where new products for cats can be promoted. It is the only event in which you have the opportunity of seeing just about every color and pattern variety that exists in the Abyssinian breed.

Even if you have no plans to become a breeder or exhibitor, you should visit at least one or two cat shows to see what a quality Abyssinian looks like.

## TYPES OF SHOW

Shows range from the small informal affairs that attract a largely local entry to the major all-breed championships and specialty exhibitions that can be spread over two or more days (but only one in Britain). A specialty is a show restricted either by breed or by hair length (short or long). In the US, it is quite common for two or more shows to run concurrently at the same site.

## SHOW CLASSES

The number of classes staged at a given show will obviously reflect its size, but the classes fall into various major divisions. These are championships for whole cats,

Exhibiting your Aby can be exciting and challenging. And even if you don't finish as well as you had hoped to, you still will have had the opportunity to meet new friends who share your interest in the breed.

The overall impression of the ideal Abyssinian is a colorful cat with a distinctly ticked coat, medium in size, and regal in appearance.

premierships for altered cats, open classes for both of the previous cats, kittens, and household pets. In all but the pet class, there are separate classes for males and females. There are then classes for all of the color and pattern varieties. At a small show, the color/patterns may be grouped into fewer classes than at a major show.

All classes are judged against the standard for the breed, other than pet classes, in which the exhibits are judged on the basis of condition and general appeal, or uniqueness of pattern. An unregistered Abyssinian can be entered into a pet class, and it will be judged on the same basis as would a mixed breed. A kitten in the US is a cat of four months of age but under eight months on the day of a show. In Britain a kitten is a cat of three or more months and under nine months on the show day.

## AWARDS AND PRIZES

The major awards in cats are those of Champion and Grand Champion, Premier and Grand Premier. In Britain, a cat must win three challenge certificates under different judges to become a champion, while in the US it must win six winner's ribbons. In both instances, these awards are won via the open class. Once a cat is a champion, it then competes in the champions' class and becomes a grand based on points earned in defeating other champions. The prizes can range from certificates, ribbons and cups to trophies and cash.

Wins in kitten classes do not count toward champion status. Champion status in one association does not carry over to another, in which a cat would have to win its title again based on the rules of that association. The rules of competition are complex, and any would-be exhibitor should obtain a copy of them from their particular registry.

The general format of cat shows, while differing somewhat from one country to another, is much the same in broad terms. An Abyssinian will enter its color or pattern class. If it wins, it will progress to compete against other group winners in its breed, and ultimately compete for best of breed. If classes have been scheduled for all of the recognized colors and patterns in all of the recognized breeds, then a Best in Show will be the ultimate award. This is the dream of every cat exhibitor.

## JUDGING

As stated earlier, cats are judged against their written standard rather than against each other. A winning cat is one that records the highest total of points, or, put another way, the least number of demerit marks. In the US, cats are taken to the judge's table for assessment, but in Britain the judge moves around the pens with a trolley. In the US, judging is done in front of the public, but in the UK judging is normally done before the public is allowed into the hall. The exhibit owners are requested to leave the hall during judging.

## CAT PENS

When you arrive at the cat show, a pen will be allocated to your cat. This is an all-wire cage. In Britain, the rules governing what can be placed into the cage are very rigid. This is because there can be no means of identifying the owner of the cat when the judge arrives at that pen. Thus, the blanket, the litter box and the water vessel must all be white. In the US the pens are highly decorated with silks, gorgeous

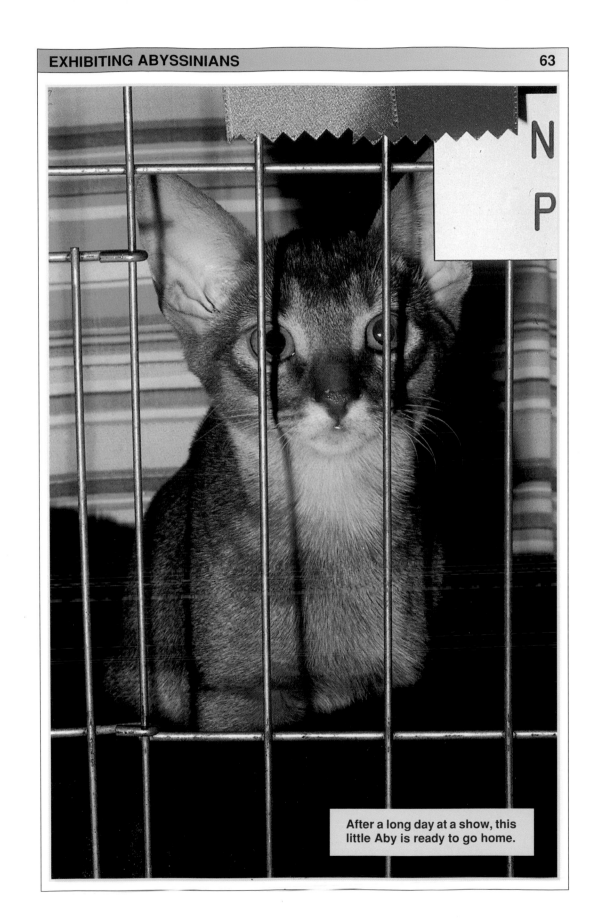

After a long day at a show, this little Aby is ready to go home.

cushions, and so on because the cat is taken to another pen for judging.

## THE EXHIBITION ABYSSINIAN

Obviously, an Abyssinian show cat must be a very sound example of its breed. Its coat must be in truly beautiful condition because the level of competition is extremely high at the major events. At more local affairs, the quality will not be as high, which gives more exhibitors a chance to pick up victories in the absence of the top cats of the country. The male cat must have two descended testicles and have a valid vaccination certificate against feline enteritis that was issued at least seven days before the show. It should have tested negative for feline leukemia (and/or any other diseases as required by your registry).

A show cat must be well-mannered because if it should bite or claw the judge, it is hardly likely to win favor. It could even be disqualified, depending on the regulations of your registry. In any case, such a cat could not be examined properly by the judge, so this alone would preclude it from any hope of winning. It must therefore become accustomed to such treatment by being handled very often as a kitten by friends and relatives.

## ENTERING A SHOW

You must apply to the show secretary for an entry blank and a schedule. The secretary will list the classes and state the rules of that association. The entry form must be completed and returned, with fees due, by the last date of entry as stipulated for that show. It is very important that you enter the correct classes; otherwise, your cat will be eliminated and your fee forfeited. If you are unsure about this aspect, you can seek the advice of an exhibitor of your acquaintance, or simply call the show secretary, who will advise you.

## SHOW ITEMS

When attending a show you will need a variety of items. They include a cat carrier, litter box, blankets, food and water vessels, food, your cat's own supply of your local water if necessary, disinfectant, first aid kit, grooming tools, paper towels, entry pass, vaccination certificates, show catalog to check the entry for your cat and when it is likely to be judged, a small stool, and decorations for the pen. You may also wish to take your own food. Indeed, it would be wise to invest in a collapsible cart or trolley to transport all of the above!

The best advice is that you should visit shows and talk with exhibitors so that you can get the feel of things before you make the plunge yourself. Showing is a fascinating and thoroughly addictive pastime, but it is also time-consuming, can be costly, and entails a great deal of dedication. Fortunately, you can participate to whatever level you wish. You are also assured of making many new friends in the process.

# INDEX